The MATHSKETEERS

A Mental-Maths Adventure

Illustrated by John Bigwood

Written and edited by Jonny Leighton

Designed by Jack Clucas and John Bigwood

Educational Consultancy by Kirstin Swanson

Buster Books

Addio

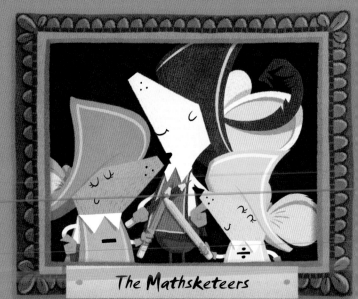

The Mathsketeers

Addio is a young noblemouse looking for a mental-maths adventure. He wants to be just like his heroes, the famous Mathsketeers — Subtractus, Multiplus and Diviso — mousematicians to the King.

But along the way he'll meet Count Catulus, a cunning cat who wants to steal the throne. Can you use your maths skills to help Addio become a Mathsketeer and save the kingdom?

Count Catulus

The challenges in this book are organized into the following sections:

NOVICE
BASIC MENTAL ADDITION

Addio wants to be just like his heroes, the Mathsketeers. He's always doing mental maths, even if it's just adding up the things lying around his room.

Eg 2 socks + 3 socks = 5 socks

PUZZLE 1:

Add up the pencils on Addio's desk. How many are there in total?

PUZZLE 2:

Addio loves a snack when he's adding up. Add together the pieces of fruit.

TOP TIP

When adding together more than two numbers, it can help to break up the sums into different parts. For example, if you want to add:

$$5 + 8 + 4$$

First, add 5 + 8 to get 13.

Then add 13 + 4 to get 17.

QUICK QUIZ:

Finish Addio's homework.

3 + 4 + 5 = ...   8 + 7 + 2 = ...

6 + 4 + 7 = ...   4 + 5 + 9 = ...

4 + 9 + 6 = ...   3 + 5 + 7 = ...

3 + 3 + 3 = ...   8 + 4 + 6 = ...

DAILY ✦ MOUSE

PUZZLE 3:

Addio reads about the Mathsketeers in the newspaper.
They're doing impressive maths sums for King Leopaw, adding
numbers with one, two and three digits. Can you do these sums, too?

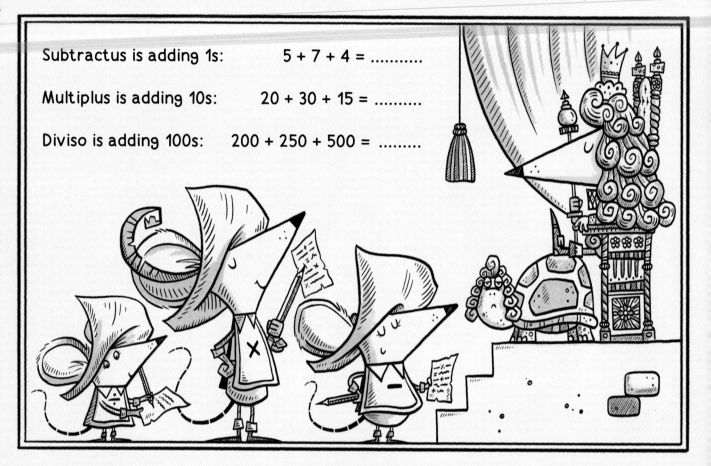

Subtractus is adding 1s: 5 + 7 + 4 = ...

Multiplus is adding 10s: 20 + 30 + 15 = ...

Diviso is adding 100s: 200 + 250 + 500 = ...

PUZZLE 4:

Addio's favourite part of the newspaper is the puzzle page. Can you help
him work out the solutions to these number basket challenges below?

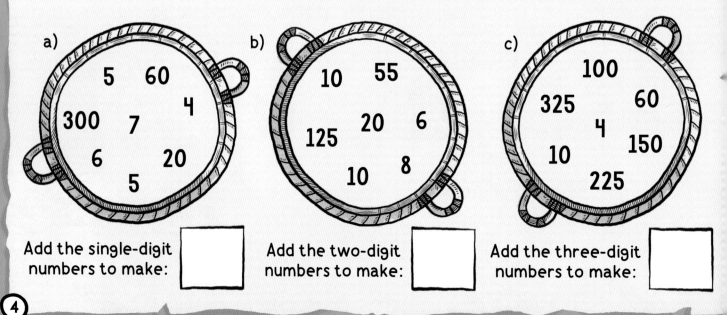

a)
5   60
300   4
7
6   20
5

b)
10   55
20   6
125
10   8

c)
100
325   60
4
10   150
225

Add the single-digit
numbers to make: ☐

Add the two-digit
numbers to make: ☐

Add the three-digit
numbers to make: ☐

BASIC MENTAL SUBTRACTION

Addio is going to Paris to meet the Mathsketeers for himself, but he's packed his bags with far too much stuff. No one needs ten toothbrushes! Can you help him subtract the things he doesn't need?

10 toothbrushes   9 toothbrushes   1 toothbrush

PUZZLE 5:

It's not just toothbrushes Addio's packed too many of. Complete these subtraction calculations to work out how many of each thing he needs.

$11 - 3 =$ .... T-shirts

$16 - 7 =$ .... notebooks

$19 - 4 =$ .... blocks of cheese

Addio started with 46 items and has got rid of 14. How many has he got left in total?

PUZZLE 6:

No matter how hard he tries, Addio's bag can only fit 15 items. He'll have to leave some behind.

Subtract 15 from his total. How many items will Addio have to leave out?

PUZZLE 7:

Paris is 100 kilometres away by road, but there are shortcuts which will reduce Addio's journey. Work out how far each route would be.

TOP TIP

When subtracting more than one number, it might help to group some together, first. Eg:

$100 - 25 - 13 = ?$

1st step: $25 + 13 = 38$

2nd step: $100 - 38 = 62$

a) A trip down the river by boat will take off 22 kilometres and asking the captain for help will take off an extra 14.

b) A trip through the forest will take off 17 kilometres and following the bumblebee trail will take off an extra 25.

c) A trip over the mountains will take off 15 kilometres and skiing down the other side will take off an extra 12.

The shortest route is: ....

QUICK ADDITION AND SUBTRACTION QUIZ:

Addio needs a rest. He sits down to catch his breath and practise his mental maths. Complete this quick addition and subtraction quiz.

$8 + 4 + 5 = $ .... $25 - 15 - 2 = $ ....

$19 + 17 + 3 = $ .... $42 - 10 - 12 = $ ....

$10 + 22 + 12 = $ .... $77 - 17 - 15 = $ ....

$50 + 5 + 30 = $ .... $90 - 23 - 14 = $ ....

NUMBER LINES

On the road just outside Paris, Addio is pickpocketed by a pesky cat. Can you help him win a number line contest to regain his possessions? The person who finishes the number line first will be the winner.

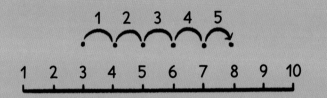

1   2   3   4   5

1   2   3   4   5   6   7   8   9   10

TOP TIP
Number lines help visualize addition and subtraction sums. Eg: if you want to add 5 to 3 on this line, just count out the notches and see where you end up.

PUZZLE 8:

Follow the instructions on each of the number lines to work out where Addio finishes. Be aware that they each go up in different increments. When you're done, why not create your own number line and challenge a friend to a duel? See who can do the quickest calculations.

a) Start at 1. Add 8, subtract 4, then add 5. Circle where you end up on the line.

1   2   3   4   5   6   7   8   9   10

a) Start at 15. Add 30, subtract 15, then add 25. Circle where you end up on the line.

15   20   25   30   35   40   45   50   55   60

c) Start at 125. Add 100, subtract 75, then add 150. Circle where you end up on the line.

125   150   175   200   225   250   275   300

NUMBER ORDERING

It's late at night and Addio finally arrives at the Paris city gates.
He's greeted by a door-mouse who needs to untangle his jumble of
keys before he lets Addio in. Putting numbers in the right order will help.

PUZZLE 9:

Each key has a number on it. Can you untangle
the keys and put them in the spaces below,
in order, from lowest to highest?

....

441   628   414   206   215   682   144   252

PUZZLE 10:

The door-mouse can't quite remember which key will open the door, but
he does remember that: "It's not the largest number, nor the smallest.
It doesn't begin with a 2 and it doesn't end with a 1, and it is a
three-digit number made up of three different numbers."

Which key is it? ....

PUZZLE 11:

Addio picks the right key and is let into Paris. Now, he needs to work out where the Mathsketeers live. They've left a fiendish puzzle at the gate for anyone worthy enough to find them. Only one calculation matches to a real house number on this street. Which one is it?

TOP TIP

Use 'partitioning' to help break up numbers that are difficult to add into 1s, 10s and 100s. Eg:

450 + 96 becomes

450 + 90 + 6

a) 115 + 53 = ...

b) 256 + 87 = ...

c) 435 + 44 = ...

d) 606 + 79 = ...

e) 222 + 22 = ...

f) 714 + 66 = ...

The right house is number:

....

665

244

477

166

340

781

THE BIG TEST:

Addio has arrived at the house, but when he knocks on the door, the Mathsketeers make him do a mega sum to gain entry. Help Addio and complete the Novice section.

10 + 15 = ... − 3 = ...

+ 125 = ... − 17 = ...

+ 44 = ... − 23 =

....

9

APPRENTICE
BASIC MENTAL MULTIPLICATION

Addio finally gets to meet his heroes, Subtracto, Diviso and Multiplus, the three Mathsketeers. He soon discovers that they like nothing better than to show off to each other and brag about their multiplication skills.

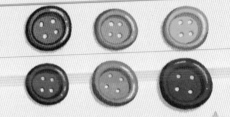

PUZZLE 1:

Subtracto shows off the special medals she's received from the King. There are three lots of three medals, or 3 x 3. Write how many medals there are in the box.

PUZZLE 2:

Diviso shows off all the special gold coins she received as payment for her latest escapade. There are three lots of five coins, or 3 x 5. Write how many coins she has in the box.

PUZZLE 3:

Multiplus lays out some food for their guest. There are four lots of three snacks, or 4 x 3. Write how many snacks there are in the box.

PUZZLE 4:

The Mathsketeers will agree to take Addio on as an apprentice — if he impresses them with his times-table skills first. Can you fill in the tables below, and help Addio become an apprentice Mathsketeer?

1 x 3 = ...	1 x 4 = ...	1 x 5 = ...
2 x 3 = ...	2 x 4 = ...	2 x 5 = ...
3 x 3 = ...	3 x 4 = ...	3 x 5 = ...
4 x 3 = ...	4 x 4 = ...	4 x 5 = ...
5 x 3 = ...	5 x 4 = ...	5 x 5 = ...
6 x 3 = ...	6 x 4 = ...	6 x 5 = ...
7 x 3 = ...	7 x 4 = ...	7 x 5 = ...
8 x 3 = ...	8 x 4 = ...	8 x 5 = ...
9 x 3 = ...	9 x 4 = ...	9 x 5 = ...
10 x 3 = ...	10 x 4 = ...	10 x 5 = ...
11 x 3 = ...	11 x 4 = ...	11 x 5 = ...
12 x 3 = ...	12 x 4 = ...	12 x 5 = ...

TOP TIP

If you're struggling, try using arrays, as shown on the previous page. They can help you to visualize tricky multiplications.

You don't have to use coins or medals like the Mathsketeers, you can use whatever you like!

PUZZLE 5:

The three Mathsketeers officially accept Addio as an apprentice.
The first thing they need to do is to present him to King Leopaw.
He's in his throne room, which can only be accessed by going through
rooms with numbers in the three-times table. Guide the Mathsketeers
through the rooms, but be warned, the numbers aren't in the right order.

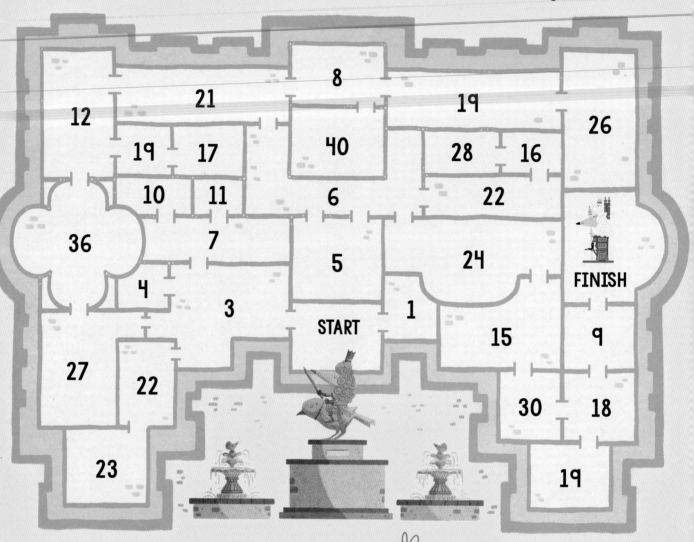

THE KING'S QUIZ:

They make it to the King's throne room.
If Addio can complete one final test,
Leopaw will present him with his
special Mathsketeer outfit and pencil.

3 x 9 = ...   8 x 3 = ...

7 x 4 = ...   3 x 12 = ...

8 x 5 = ...   4 x 8 = ...

PUZZLE 6:

One of the King's courtiers interrupts the ceremony — some of the precious crown jewels have gone missing! Can you work out how many of each type of jewel has disappeared? The King's Keeper of the Jewels has an inventory of everything that should be there.

Diamonds:
There should be six rings, each with three diamonds on them.

6 rings x 3 diamonds = ... diamonds

Rubies:
There should be six necklaces, each with eight rubies on them.

6 necklaces x 8 rubies = ... rubies

Emeralds:
There should be seven brooches, each with five emeralds on them.

7 brooches x 5 emeralds =

.... emeralds

PUZZLE 7:

Worst of all, one of King Leopaw's crowns has gone missing, too. There are seven points to it, each with three sapphires on them. How many sapphires are there in total?

....

Addio and the Mathsketeers find a clue: a piece of fur snagged on one of the palace windows. It could only have come from a cat!

BASIC MENTAL DIVISION

The King orders the Mathsketeers and Addio to find out who the cat hair belongs to and to recover the precious jewels right away.
They'll have to use basic mental division to do it.

INVERSE OPERATIONS

You can think of division as the opposite of multiplication, in the same way that subtraction is the opposite of addition. They are 'inverse' operations.

For example:

$3 \times 2 = 6$

is the inverse operation of

$6 \div 2 = 3$

PUZZLE 8:

There were eight witnesses that saw suspicious activity in the palace.
The four mice decide to interview an equal number of them.

8 witnesses ÷ 4 mice = ... interviews each

MAP MUDDLE:

On a map of Paris, there are 20 zones that need investigating. They divide them between the four of them. How many zones do they study each?

....

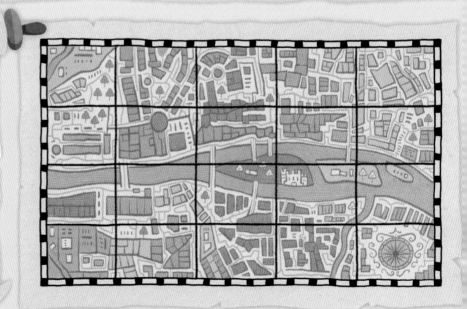

QUICK DIVISION QUIZ:

Before they leave the palace, Addio wants to put his division skills to the test. Complete this quick division quiz, dividing by 2, 3 and 4.

10 ÷ 2 = ...   16 ÷ 4 = ...

9 ÷ 3 = ...   24 ÷ 3 = ...

12 ÷ 4 = ...   22 ÷ 2 = ...

18 ÷ 2 = ...   33 ÷ 3 = ...

PUZZLE 9:

The mice follow the clues they've discovered and track down a gang of alley cats they believe to have stolen the jewels. Unfortunately, they're outnumbered. Add the answers to these division questions to the spaces, to find out which pipes go where, helping them escape.

c) 40 ÷ 4

d) 27 ÷ 3

b) 25 ÷ 5

e) 24 ÷ 2

a) 18 ÷ 3

f) 32 ÷ 4

PUZZLE 10:

The Mathsketeers and Addio escape to the rooftops, but the danger's not over. They need to get back home, but they MUST avoid buildings that cats live in. Cats live in buildings with answers greater than 7.

a) 25 ÷ 5

b) 75 ÷ 25

c) 40 ÷ 4

d) 24 ÷ 3

e) 15 ÷ 5

g) 36 ÷ 6

h) 200 ÷ 100

f) 12 ÷ 1

l) 50 ÷ 10

i) 16 ÷ 2

j) 27 ÷ 3

k) 30 ÷ 5

HOME

The Mathsketeers must avoid houses: ....

PRIME PROBLEM:

Some numbers can only be divided by themselves and one, and still give a whole number. These are called prime numbers.

For example, 3 can only be divided by 3 (to give 1) and 1 (to give 3). Whereas 4 can be divided by itself, 2 and 1.

There are four prime numbers between one and ten. What are they?

....

....

PUZZLE 11:

Addio and the Mathsketeers make it safely back to their home. Addio reveals a piece of paper he swiped from one of the alley cats. It says that the cats are working for a prominent noble cat in Paris, who wants to take King Leopaw's crown and throne for their own. Can you work out which cat it is?

The number chain with the highest answer at the end represents the villain behind the robbery.

WANTED
FOR QUESTIONING

18 —+ 92→ ○ —- 10→ ○ —÷ 4→ ○ —x 5→ ○

COUNT CATULUS

54 —÷ 6→ ○ —x 10→ ○ —- 16→ ○ —+ 50→ ○

GENERAL WHISKERLESS

60 —÷ 10→ ○ —x 6→ ○ —+ 90→ ○ —- 9→ ○

MADAME POMPAPAW

Addio works out that .... is the villain behind the robbery. It's going to take all the mice's maths powers to catch the villain and recover the jewels. Addio is promoted to full Mathsketeer status.

MATHSKETEER
MONEY MATHS

Before they get to work finding
Count Catulus, Addio needs to look the
part of a fully-fledged Mathsketeer.
It's time to go shopping.

PUZZLE 1:

Before going to the shops, work out how
much money the mice have got to spend.

Addio has:

£5   50P   20P   50P   2P   20P   1P   20P   £1   1P   2P

Subtracto has:

£10   20P   5P   50P   10P   2P   2P   £5   2P   £1

Multiplus has:

£10   20P   £1   2P   1P   50P   2P   £5   20P

Diviso has:

£1   1P   2P   20P   20P   £10   2P   50P   5P   £1

PUZZLE 2:

How much money
do the mice
have in total?

....

PUZZLE 3:

Subtracto thinks it's best to leave
some money at home. They take £50
with them. How much do they leave?

....

PUZZLE 4:

Addio needs a new hat, a new notebook to do his sums and a new pair of boots. How much would they all cost if he bought the cheapest? And how much would they all cost if he bought the most expensive?

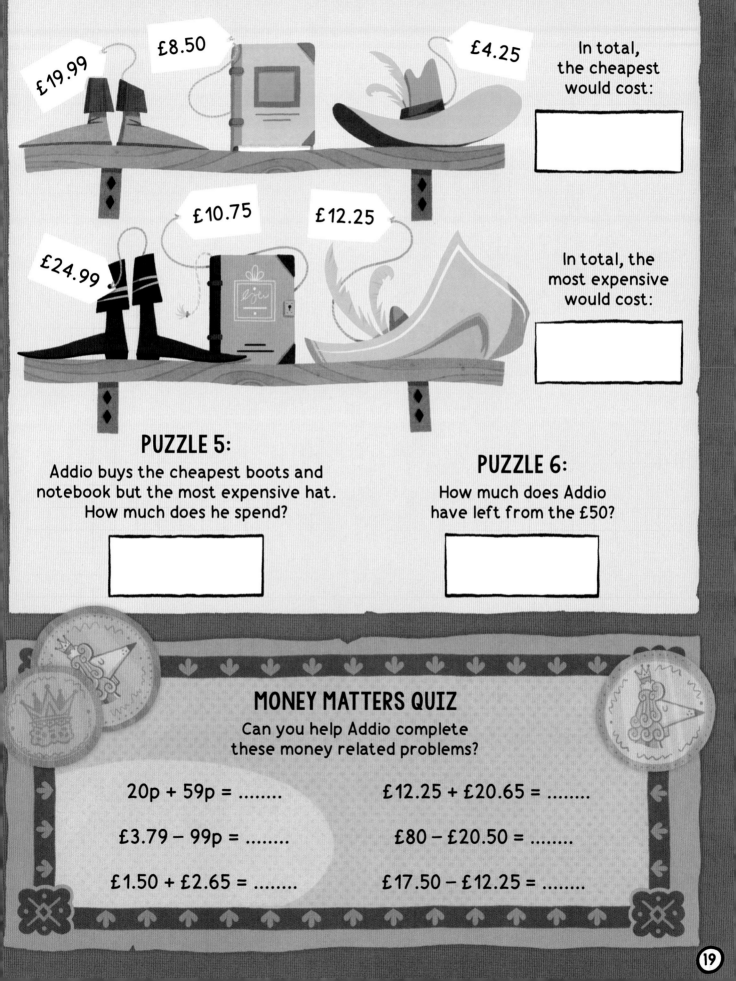

£8.50

£19.99

£4.25

In total, the cheapest would cost:

£10.75

£12.25

£24.99

In total, the most expensive would cost:

PUZZLE 5:

Addio buys the cheapest boots and notebook but the most expensive hat. How much does he spend?

PUZZLE 6:

How much does Addio have left from the £50?

MONEY MATTERS QUIZ

Can you help Addio complete these money related problems?

20p + 59p = ...

£12.25 + £20.65 = ...

£3.79 − 99p = ...

£80 − £20.50 = ...

£1.50 + £2.65 = ...

£17.50 − £12.25 = ...

FACTOR PAIRS

The Mathsketeers are on the trail of Count Catulus's hideout. First, they have to get across the choppy river waters using their knowledge of factor pairs.

PUZZLE 7:

On the left bank there are seven boats with factor pairs and on the right there are seven landing stages with answers. Can you match them up?

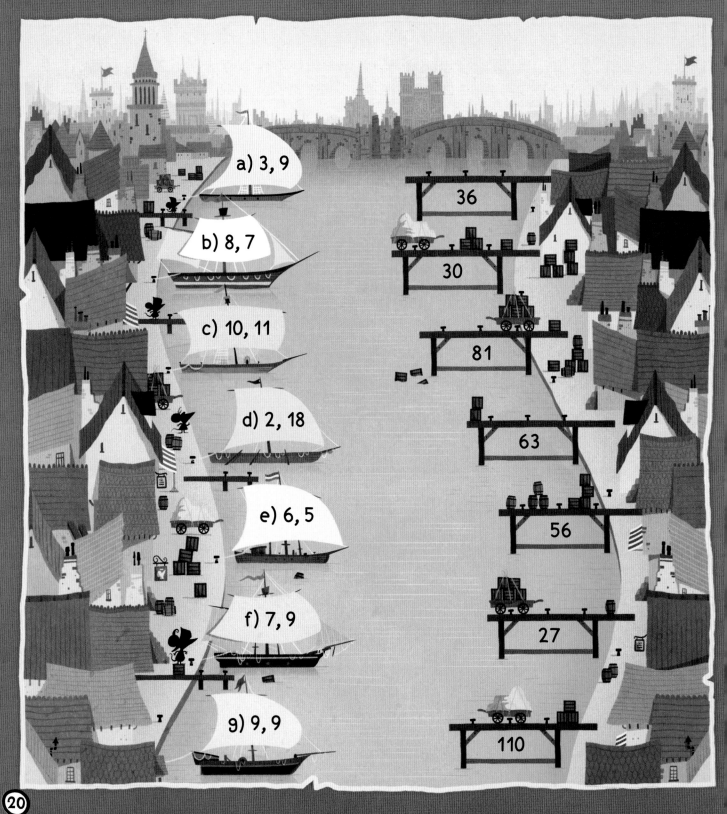

a) 3, 9

b) 8, 7

c) 10, 11

d) 2, 18

e) 6, 5

f) 7, 9

g) 9, 9

36

30

81

63

56

27

110

PUZZLE 8:

Numbers can have lots of factor pairs. For example, the number 12 has 3: 1 and 12, 2 and 6, and 3 and 4. Count Catulus has left his calling card at one of the jetties, but only for those who know their factor pairs. Catulus's card is the one where all the pairs of numbers are factor pairs of the address. Which one is it?

50 RUE DE FROMAGE

10, 5	2, 25
3, 17	1, 50

24 Hotel Moustaches

2, 12	24, 1
3, 8	13, 2

64 Maison de la Souris

2, 26	8, 8	16, 4	64, 1

36 Boulevard de Patte

6, 6	18, 2
3, 12	8, 4

48 Chateau de Chat

6, 8	3, 16	4, 12	2, 24

Count Catulus lives at: ....

FRACTION ACTION

The Mathsketeers are heading for the Chateau de Chat to confront Count Catulus. First, though, they stop off at a restaurant for some lunch. Chef Gaston le Gourmand is in a muddle with his bread and cheese. Can you help him match the fractions?

PUZZLE 9:

Match loaves of bread with blocks of cheese that have the same fractions remaining.

a) $\dfrac{6}{8}$

b) $\dfrac{2}{3}$

c) $\dfrac{2}{6}$

d) $\dfrac{5}{10}$

e) $\dfrac{1}{3}$

f) $\dfrac{4}{6}$

g) $\dfrac{3}{4}$

h) $\dfrac{6}{12}$

TOP TIP
Some fractions have the same value as each other. For example $\frac{1}{2}$ is the same as $\frac{2}{4}$.

PUZZLE 10:

According to Gaston, Catulus's home has 12 guards. But they're not all on duty at the same time. The Mathsketeers keep a close watch on the castle for a full day. Count the cats to find out what fraction of them are on guard at each time of day.

a) Morning

b) Midday

c) Sunset

d) Night

a) ☐ / 12   b) ☐ / 12   c) ☐ / 12   d) ☐ / 12

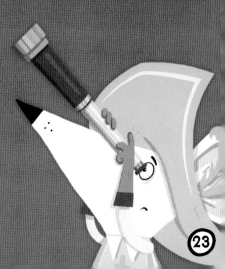

According to Gaston, the best time to sneak in is when $\frac{3}{4}$ of the guards are there. Even though there are more guards than at some other times, they don't guard the side entrance. When should the Mathsketeers sneak in?

....

SEQUENCES

The Mathsketeers sneak into Count Catulus's home. He loves maths and numbers — everything in his house is in a sequence. Sequences can help identify patterns between numbers, like this:

2, 4, 6, 8, 10, 12, 14, 16 ...

These numbers all go up by two every time. As the Mathsketeers sneak around Catulus's home to try and find the jewels that he stole, can you work out the sequences they see along the way?

PUZZLE 11:

a) Catulus has many noble ancestors. Which numbers are missing?

Henri 3rd

Marie 6th

Max .....

Josef 12th

Georges ......

b) The Mathsketeers have to get to the door at the end of the corridor. What number should be on the doors?

35   28   21   ....

PUZZLE 12:

The Mathsketeers have found Catulus's safe room.
The stolen crown jewels must be in here. Complete the
sequences on the combination locks to open the safe.

a)

| 8 | ..... | 24 | ..... | 40 |

b)

| 66 | 56 | 47 | 39 | ..... |

c)

| 1 | 6 | 11 | 16 | ..... |

d)

| 160 | 80 | 40 | 20 | ..... |

Add up all the missing numbers
to find the final number that
will open the vault.

....

The Mathsketeers found
the King's precious jewels.
They're sure to be legends
across the kingdom. Now
they just have to get
out of there!

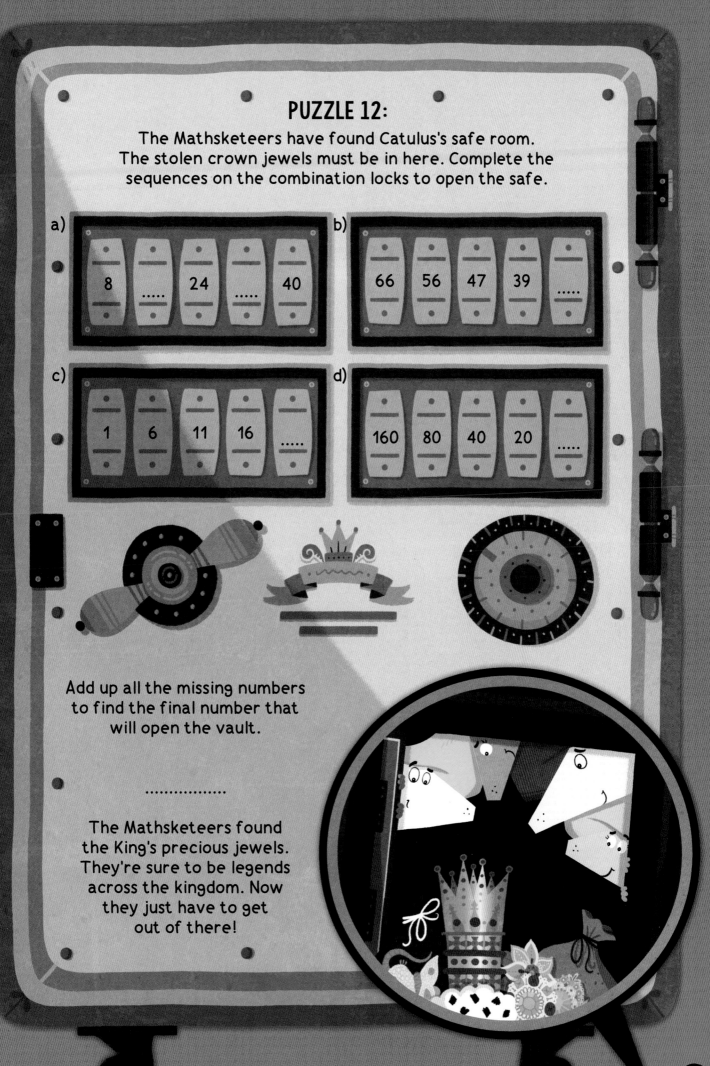

LEGEND
MISSING NUMBERS

Count Catulus has discovered the Mathsketeers in his safe room. He knew they'd come — the theft of the jewels was a trick to bring them here.

"I'm the greatest mathematician in the land," he boasts. "And without you around to help the King, I'm going to take the throne for myself!"

PUZZLE 1:

Count Catulus proves just what a smarty pants he is by doing missing number calculations. Can you work out which numbers are missing, too?

$$45 + a = 56$$

a = ...

$$23 - b = 7$$

b = ...

$$7 \times c = 77$$

c = ...

$$120 \div d = 60$$

d = ...

PUZZLE 2:

Count Catulus locks the Mathsketeers up in the dungeons beneath his house. He's off to the King's palace to challenge him for the throne. The Mathsketeers must act fast to help King Leopaw before it's too late. Help the Mathsketeers find the weakness in the cell's bars. The letter with the lowest value corresponds to the weakest bar.

a)
$$24 + a = 36$$

b)
$$45 \div b = 5$$

c)
$$68 - c = 44$$

d)
$$10 \times d = 50$$

a = ...

b = ...

c = ...

d = ...

The Mathsketeers need to break bar: ....

SUPER-HARD CALCULATIONS

The Mathsketeers have escaped the dungeon and are off to the palace to protect the King. First they'll have to cross Paris, really fast.

$$
\begin{array}{r}
\text{H T O} \\
1\,9\,8 \\
+\,2_1 1_1 3 \\
\hline
4\,1\,1
\end{array}
$$

Column methods help when you're adding or subtracting large numbers. Start by solving the ones column, then move on to the tens column and the hundreds column.

PUZZLE 3:

Each cart has a different rating based on the speed and skill of the rider and horse. Which one has the highest rating? If the numbers in the ones or tens column add up to more than 10, you will have to carry them across to the next column.

a)
$$
\begin{array}{r}
4\,2\,5 \\
+\,3\,1\,5 \\
\hline
\end{array}
$$
....

b)
$$
\begin{array}{r}
6\,0\,6 \\
+\,6\,1\,6 \\
\hline
\end{array}
$$
....

c)
$$
\begin{array}{r}
2\,4\,5 \\
+\,4\,0\,5 \\
\hline
\end{array}
$$
....

d)
$$
\begin{array}{r}
4\,4\,4 \\
+\,5\,1\,5 \\
\hline
\end{array}
$$
....

e)
$$
\begin{array}{r}
1\,2\,4 \\
+\,2\,9\,5 \\
\hline
\end{array}
$$
....

f)
$$
\begin{array}{r}
3\,9\,3 \\
+\,1\,0\,1 \\
\hline
\end{array}
$$
....

The best cart is: ....

PUZZLE 4:

While racing through the streets, Addio and the Mathsketeers take the chance to brush up on their subtraction skills.

a)
$$926$$
$$-311$$
....

b)
$$488$$
$$-123$$
....

c)
$$879$$
$$-521$$
....

d)
$$333$$
$$-111$$
....

e)
$$439$$
$$-338$$
....

f)
$$755$$
$$-424$$
....

EXTRA-TRICKY QUIZ

See if you can complete these extra-tricky big sums without using columns.

230 + 170 = ...   100 − 42 = ...

110 + 135 = ...   220 − 175 = ...

440 + 268 = ...   305 − 113 = ...

THE BIG ROUNDUP

The Mathsketeers arrive at the palace to find Count Catulus in a fearsome number showdown with the King.

PUZZLE 5:

Can you use some of the skills you've learned throughout the journey to help the King defeat Count Catulus?

MISSING NUMBERS

a) $230 + a = 273$

a = ...

b) $60 \div b = 12$

b = ...

c) $5 \times c = 35$

c = ...

SEQUENCES

d) $\frac{1}{2}, \frac{1}{4}, \frac{1}{6}, \frac{1}{8}$ ....

e) 800, 400, 200, 100 ....

f) 12, 15, 21, 30 ....

MONEY MATHS

g) £2.50 x 3 = ...

h) £6.99 + £8.99 = ...

i) £12.99 − £4.50 = ...

PUZZLE 6:

The King needs help from his trusty Mathsketeers.
Help them as they step in to defeat Count Catulus.

FACTOR PAIRS

a) Give the three
factor pairs of 16.

....

b) Give the three
factor pairs of 28.

....

c) Give the four
factor pairs of 40.

....

....

CONGRATULATIONS!

Success! The Mathsketeers' amazing maths skills
have seen off Count Catulus. As a token of
his thanks, the King awards the four
mice a shiny new medal.

ANSWERS

NOVICE

Puzzle 1
7 + 6 = 13

Puzzle 2
3 + 8 = 11

Quick Quiz
3 + 4 + 5 = 12
6 + 4 + 7 = 17
4 + 9 + 6 = 19
3 + 3 + 3 = 9
8 + 7 + 2 = 17
4 + 5 + 9 = 18
3 + 5 + 7 = 15
8 + 4 + 6 = 18

Puzzle 3
5 + 7 + 4 = 16
20 + 30 + 15 = 65
200 + 250 + 500 = 950

Puzzle 4
a) 7 + 4 + 5 + 5 + 6 = 27
b) 10 + 55 + 20 + 10 = 95
c) 100 + 325 + 150 + 225 = 800

Puzzle 5
11 − 3 = 8

16 − 7 = 9
19 − 4 = 15

Addio has got 32 items left in total.

Puzzle 6
32 items − 15 spaces = 17 items that Addio will have to leave out.

Puzzle 7
a) 100 − 22 − 14 = 64 kilometres
b) 100 − 17 − 25 = 58 kilometres
c) 100 − 15 − 12 = 73 kilometres

The shortest route is b, 58 kilometres.

Quick Addition and Subtraction Quiz
8 + 4 + 5 = 17
19 + 17 + 3 = 39
10 + 22 + 12 = 44
50 + 5 + 30 = 85
25 − 15 − 2 = 8
42 − 10 − 12 = 20
77 − 17 − 15 = 45
90 − 23 − 14 = 53

Puzzle 8
a) 10
b) 55
c) 300

Puzzle 9
The order is: 144, 206, 215, 252, 414, 441, 628, 682

Puzzle 10
The correct key is number 628.

Puzzle 11
a) 115 + 53 = 168
b) 256 + 87 = 343
c) 435 + 44 = 479
d) 606 + 79 = 685
e) 222 + 22 = 244
f) 714 + 66 = 780

The correct house is number 244.

The Big Test
10 + 15 = 25
25 − 3 = 22
22 + 125 = 147
147 − 17 = 130
130 + 44 = 174
174 − 23 = 151

Puzzle 10
The Mathsketeers avoid c, d, f, i, j.

Prime Problem
2, 3, 5 and 7

Puzzle 11
Count Catulus = 125

General Whiskerless = 124

Madame Pompapaw = 117

Count Catulus is the villain.

MATHSKETEER

Puzzle 1
Addio has £7.66.
Subtracto has £16.91.
Multiplus has £16.95.
Diviso has £13.

Puzzle 2
The mice have £54.52

Puzzle 3
They leave £4.52 at home.

Puzzle 4
In total, the cheapest costs £32.74.

In total, the most expensive costs £47.99.

Puzzle 5
£40.74

Puzzle 6
£9.26

Money Matters Quiz
20p + 59p = 79p
£3.79 − 99p = £2.80
£1.50 + £2.65 = £4.15
£12.25 + £20.65 = £32.90
£80 − £20.50 = £59.50
£17.50 − £12.25 = £5.25

Puzzle 7
a) 27
b) 56
c) 110
d) 36
e) 30
f) 63
g) 81

Puzzle 8
Count Catulus lives at the Chateau de Chat.

Puzzle 9
a) and g)
b) and f)
c) and e)
d) and h)

Puzzle 10
a) $\frac{8}{12}$
b) $\frac{10}{12}$
c) $\frac{6}{12}$
d) $\frac{9}{12}$

The Mathsketeers sneak in at night.

Puzzle 11
a) Max 9th and Georges 15th
b) 14 and 7

Puzzle 12
a) 8, 16, 24, 32, 40
b) 66, 56, 47, 39, 32
c) 1, 6, 11, 16, 21
d) 160, 80, 40, 20, 10

Adding up the missing numbers will give 111.

APPRENTICE

Puzzle 1
9 medals

Puzzle 2
15 coins

Puzzle 3
12 snacks

Puzzle 4
See times table square.

Puzzle 5

The King's Quiz
3 x 9 = 27
7 x 4 = 28
8 x 5 = 40
8 x 3 = 24
3 x 12 = 36
4 x 8 = 32

Puzzle 6
18 diamonds, 48 rubies and 35 emeralds

Puzzle 7
7 points x 3 sapphires = 21 sapphires on the crown

Puzzle 8
8 witnesses ÷ 4 mice = 2 interviews each

Map Muddle
They study five zones each.

Quick Division Quiz
10 ÷ 2 = 5
9 ÷ 3 = 3
12 ÷ 4 = 3
18 ÷ 2 = 9
16 ÷ 4 = 4
24 ÷ 3 = 8
22 ÷ 2 = 11
33 ÷ 3 = 11

Puzzle 9
a) 6
b) 5
c) 10
d) 9
e) 12
f) 8

LEGEND

Puzzle 1
a = 11
b = 16
c = 11
d = 2

Puzzle 2
a = 12
b = 9
c = 24
d = 5

They need to break bar d.

Puzzle 3
a) 740
b) 1222
c) 650
d) 959
e) 419
f) 494

The best cart is cart b.

Puzzle 4
a) 615
b) 365
c) 358
d) 222
e) 101
f) 331

Extra-Tricky Quiz
230 + 170 = 400
110 + 135 = 245
440 + 268 = 708
100 − 42 = 58
220 − 175 = 45
305 − 113 = 192

Puzzle 5
a) a = 43
b) b = 5
c) c = 7
d) $\frac{4}{10}$
e) 50

f) 42
g) £7.50
h) £15.98
i) £8.49

Puzzle 6
a) 1 and 16, 2 and 8, 4 and 4.
b) 1 and 28, 2 and 14, 4 and 7.
c) 1 and 40, 2 and 20, 4 and 10, 5 and 8.

TIMES TABLES SQUARE

Use this square to check your times tables.

x	1	2	3	4	5	6	7	8	9	10	11	12
1	1	2	3	4	5	6	7	8	9	10	11	12
2	2	4	6	8	10	12	14	16	18	20	22	24
3	3	6	9	12	15	18	21	24	27	30	33	36
4	4	8	12	16	20	24	28	32	36	40	44	48
5	5	10	15	20	25	30	35	40	45	50	55	60
6	6	12	18	24	30	36	42	48	54	60	66	72
7	7	14	21	28	35	42	49	56	63	70	77	84
8	8	16	24	32	40	48	56	64	72	80	88	96
9	9	18	27	36	45	54	63	72	81	90	99	108
10	10	20	30	40	50	60	70	80	90	100	110	120
11	11	22	33	44	55	66	77	88	99	110	121	132
12	12	24	36	48	60	72	84	96	108	120	132	144

First published in Great Britain in 2022 by Buster Books, an imprint of Michael O'Mara Books Limited, 9 Lion Yard, Tremadoc Road, London SW4 7NQ

Copyright © Buster Books 2022

W www.mombooks.com/buster F Buster Books T @BusterBooks I @buster_books

A CIP catalogue record for this book is available from the British Library.

ISBN: 978-1-78055-745-8

1 3 5 7 9 10 8 6 4 2

This book was printed in April 2022 by Leo Paper Products Ltd, Heshan Astros Printing Limited, Xuantan Temple Industrial Zone, Gulao Town, Heshan City, Guangdong Province, China.